Building CI/CD Pipelines

Accelerating the Code-Review-Deploy Cycle

Table of Contents

Chapter 1. Introduction

In this Special Report, we delve deep into the realm of Continuous Integration and Continuous Deployment (CI/CD) pipelines, a cornerstone of modern software development processes. This technical exploration sheds light on how CI/CD pipelines streamline and accelerate the code-review-deploy cycle, thereby enhancing the efficiency and quality of software production. Perfectly suited for both curious newcomers and seasoned technicians, this report simplifies complex concepts and uncovers powerful insights. So, whether you're just diving into DevOps or looking to refine your existing approach, this report holds valuable lessons and strategies to help you optimally utilize CI/CD pipelines and streamline tasks while minimizing potential errors.

Chapter 2. Understanding the Fundamentals of CI/CD

The importance of Continuous Integration and Continuous Deployment, often abbreviated as CI/CD, can't be understated as we progress further into the age of agile software development, DevOps, and increasingly rapid innovation cycles. This pair of practices forms the backbone of a high-velocity software development process, enabling teams to deliver updates faster, unhindered by manual processes, integration issues, and chaotic deployments.

To truly appreciate the power of CI/CD, it's essential to unpack each term and understand the underlying processes.

2.1. Continuous Integration

Continuous Integration (CI) is a development practice where developers integrate their changes into the main branch frequently, often several times a day. The primary purpose of this approach is to prevent "integration hell," a situation where developers working in isolation on different features face numerous merge conflicts and bugs when combining their code.

In contrast, CI encourages developers to regularly push small changes to the main branch, where multiple automated checks are in place. These checks commonly include unit tests, integration tests, and static code analyses, ensuring an early detection of integration problems or bugs. The key benefits of adopting CI include reduced integration problems, less time spent on debugging, improved code quality, and faster development cycles.

Fully setting up a CI environment requires certain core principles: * Developers should merge their changes as often as possible, preferably multiple times a day. * Each integration should be verified through rigorous automated testing. * The concept should be inclusive "Build the system" and not just "Compile the code." * Everyone should be able to see the results of the latest build. * Developers should maintain a fast and fix-first approach towards fixing broken builds.

2.2. Continuous Deployment

Continuous Deployment (CD), often coupled with Continuous Delivery, is the natural extension of CI, where the code changes made in the system are automatically built, tested, and prepared for release to production. This means that a developer's changes can go live just after a successful build and test phase.

Continuous Deployment's ultimate goal is to make releasing new changes as swift as possible. It does this by cutting out several manual steps from the process - steps that encompass testing, staging, and releasing software.

Continuous Delivery vs. Continuous Deployment: In Continuous Delivery, every modification passes through the standard pipeline and produces a release candidate, which, depending on your business needs, can be manually pushed to production. In contrast, Continuous Deployment fully automates the process, where every change passes all stages of the production pipeline and is released to the customers.

The benefits of implementing CD are numerous. It not only considerably decreases the lead time to release but also increases the reliability and quality of the software being delivered. With CD, developers can respond faster to market demands and deliver value incrementally, keeping stakeholders more engaged.

In implementing CD, developers should remember: * Emphasize test automation and reliability since any failure could directly impact the customer experience. * Make deployments predictable and routine, minimizing software release anxiety. * Keep production ready code in the repository at all times. * Implement toggle features to manage new releases. * Make the deployment process repeatable and reliable by following patterns and practices that reduce errors and downtime.

2.3. The CI/CD Pipeline

The CI/CD pipeline is designed to ensure that software can be developed, tested, integrated, and deployed smoothly without causing major obstructions. A typical CI/CD pipeline comprises several stages, including:

1. **Code**: The product's codebase is developed, frequently updated, and version controlled.

2. **Build**: The code, upon integration, is compiled into an executable file.

3. **Test**: Automated tests are carried out to ensure the build is error-free.

4. **Release**: The approved build is tagged for release.

5. **Deploy**: The build is deployed to a production (or similar) environment.

6. **Operate**: The software is monitored for performance and reliability metrics.

7. **Monitor**: If issues are identified, they are fixed, and the cycle repeats.

These stages ensure that every change hitting production is bug-free, stable, and adds value to your product.

2.4. The Power of Automation

Both CI and CD rely heavily on automation to enable frequent deployments. Automated builds and automated tests reduce the manual effort required, making the whole process more reliable and far quicker. This, in turn, increases not only productivity but also the number of new features that can be added comfortably in each iteration.

Automation isn't easy to establish initially but reaps significant benefits in the long term. It requires a culture shift, with developers needing to write code that's testable and write the tests themselves - both of which can be vital in preventing late-stage issues in the software delivery cycle.

CI/CD embody a philosophy rooted in constant feedback, iterative improvement, and automation. Understanding these fundamentals allows teams to masterfully navigate a fast-paced technological landscape, delivering high-quality, reliable software releases with superior speed and efficiency.

Chapter 3. The Nuts and Bolts of Continuous Integration

Behind every successful software deployment, there's a meticulous structure that encompasses an array of practices and tools aimed at ensuring code quality, harmonizing collaborations, and safeguarding robust software deployment. This structure is formally known as Continuous Integration (CI). Broadly conceptualized, CI is a software development practice where members of a team integrate their work frequently, usually each person integrates at least daily - leading to multiple integrations per day.

3.1. The Essence of Continuous Integration

The underlying premise of Continuous Integration is clear: regular and frequent integration can reduce integration problems, which in turn allows for more time to be spent on building and enhancing the product. By integrating the output of work into a shared repository frequently, the chances of encountering conflicts and bugs decrease significantly because changes are often small and teams can address bugs quicker as the codebase is still fresh in their minds.

CI warrants that code is tested automatically and immediately, providing almost instant feedback on the system's health and the impact of the committed changes. This immediate feedback allows developers to address problems promptly, thus enhancing the software's quality and reducing the time to deliver it.

Times have changed from the days when programmers worked in solitude for extended periods before merging their work with the team. Late integrations could often take days or even weeks to align with the team's shared codebase resulting in error-prone, time-consuming processes. Today, CI emphasizes regular "commits" to the main branch, so integrations are done in real-time, ensuring aligning code changes doesn't turn into a chaotic whirlwind.

3.2. Implementing Continuous Integration

To effectively implement Continuous Integration, certain key principles and strategies should be adhered to. Esteemed software engineer Martin Fowler proposed a series of practices for effective Continuous Integration:

1. Maintain a Single Source Repository: All project assets, not just source code, should be stored in a version controlled single source repository. This ensures that each member of the team can easily access any piece of information related to the project.

2. Automate the Build: A single command should have the capability to build the system. Automating the build process ensures a repeatable and consistent procedure to retrieve the latest code from the repository, building executables, and running test suites.

3. Make Your Build Self-Testing: Implement automated tests to ensure the system works properly. Code should not only compile, but also pass tests.

4. Everyone Commits To the Mainline Every Day: To avoid the pain of integrating change sets that have diverged for a long time, everyone should integrate their changes into the mainline every day.

5. Keep the Build Fast: To provide rapid feedback, the build process should be quick. Techniques such as test selection, parallel testing, and mock objects can reduce unnecessary test running time.

6. Test in a Clone of the Production Environment: It is crucial to test

the software in an environment that resembles the production environment as much as possible. If a CI system also deploys into real production environments, it's most likely also a Continuous Deployment pipeline.

7. Make it Easy for Anyone to Get the Latest Executable: Everyone involved in the project should be able to see the system's latest working version.

8. Everyone can see what's happening: All the team can access the results of the latest build. Transparency is key to addressing problems promptly.

9. Automate Deployment: Just like the build process, deployment should be automated.

3.3. Continuous Integration in DevOps

The incorporation of Continuous Integration within a DevOps approach creates powerful synergies. DevOps - a blend of Development and Operations - is all about breaking down silos to create a collaborative environment that fosters speed and reliability in software development. Incorporating CI into a DevOps approach means bringing together the best practices of software development and IT operations, thereby enhancing the speed and quality of software production and deployment.

In CI, code is integrated, tested, and validated in a shared repository by each contributor, after which the validated code changes can be combined and deployed. With DevOps, the whole team is involved in the entire developmental cycle, meaning that it embodies not just the developers and testers but also the operations team. This joint effort thus ensures that applications are built with operational requirements in mind, reducing potential conflicts and misunderstandings.

Therefore, considering Continuous Integration when adopting a DevOps culture can be an essential enabler for consistency, efficiency, and quality control.

3.4. Walking Through a Continuous Integration Pipeline

A simple CI pipeline usually consists of the following steps:

1. Developers write code in an integrated development environment (IDE) and then commit changes to a shared version control repository (like Git). The commit then triggers the CI/CD tool.

2. Then the CI server pulls the updated code from the shared repository and builds a runtime environment (e.g., a Docker container) to run the tests.

3. Automated tests are executed. These could include small unit tests that test individual methods or functions or larger integration tests that test the system as a whole.

4. If the tests pass successfully, then the CI system might automatically deploy the code to a staging environment for further testing, or even to production if it is a continuous delivery/deployment system.

By running these steps automatically whenever someone commits code, Continuous Integration can provide rapid feedback to developers, and catch bugs when they are still small and easy to fix.

Through this report, we aim to lay a solid foundation on the principles and implementation of Continuous Integration. In the next section, we will delve into Continuous Deployment, another significant cog in the CI/CD wheel.

Chapter 4. The Power of Continuous Deployment

Crucial in software development, Continuous Deployment (CD) is a strategy that automates the process of deploying code to production environments after passing defined sets of tests. Its adoption is part of a high-performing DevOps culture, significantly improving speed, quality, and efficiency. By incorporating continuous deployment, developers are empowered to expedite product releases and swiftly accommodate client feedback, leading to higher levels of client satisfaction and improved software performance.

4.1. Defining Continuous Deployment

In the context of software development, Continuous Deployment refers to the practice of automatically deploying new code to production after succeeding through a series of automated tests. This approach is an extension of Continuous Integration, an earlier stage where code changes are regularly merged into the main repository and tested to ensure code consistency. The underlying principle is to employ automation for faster deployment with reduced error margins, thus eliminating the traditional manual deployment which is error-prone and time-consuming.

There's nestedness to this setting, wherein Continuous Deployment sits at the uppermost level, preceded by Continuous Delivery, which, in turn, sits on top of Continuous Integration.

It's worth noting that CD leverages the idea of 'fail-fast', where any identified issues during the deployment phase can be rectified quickly; the speed provided by automation allows quick recovery, minimizing the problems' effects on the live environment.

4.2. The Enabling Technologies of Continuous Deployment

The power of CD is amplified when complemented by various DevOps tools and methodologies. Here are some of the key technologies typically present in the CD environment:

1. Version Control Systems (VCS): Tools like Git help manage code changes efficiently, making it easier to track change history and revert problematic deployments if necessary.

2. Build Servers: These automate the process of generating executable applications from the source code, often taking charge of the Continuous Integration process. Examples include Jenkins and CircleCI.

3. Automated Testing Tools: These are essential for validating that code changes do not cause system failures. Examples include Selenium, Junit, and Jest.

4. Configuration Management Tools: Such as Ansible, Puppet, and Chef, they ensure that the system's configuration remains consistent across all environments, reducing deployment failures due to configuration mismatch.

5. Containerization and Orchestration Tools: Docker and Kubernetes can help manage application deployments, especially in environments that adopt Microservices Architecture.

4.3. Advantages of Continuous Deployment

Continuous deployment provides a plethora of benefits that enhance the development and deployment workflow, some of which include:

Improved Product Quality: Given the automated, comprehensive testing in place, the release quality is significantly improved. Any potential errors can be quickly detected and rectified, thereby resulting in a sturdier end product.

Faster Release Cycle: The automation of the deployment process aids in quicker and more frequent releases. This not only allows faster feature delivery but also helps in quicker client feedback loop, enabling exponential improvement.

Reduced Risk: Instead of deploying a large batch of changes, CD promotes incremental updates, thereby mitigating the risks associated with deployment. This incremental approach makes identifying and fixing problems much easier and faster.

Time Efficient: By automating manual tasks and procedures, speed is increased while the scope for human error is minimized, this makes the deployment process more efficient.

4.4. Implementing Continuous Deployment

Successful Incorporation of Continuous Deployment is a journey that involves taking the right steps guided by best practices. Here are some actionable strategies:

1. **Robust Testing Strategy**: To fully leverage the benefits of CD, a comprehensive automated testing suite involving unit testing, integration testing, and end-to-end testing is vital. It ensures that any change doesn't inadvertently break the product.

2. **Incremental Changes**: CD works best with small changes that can be easily reviewed and tested. By making changes incrementally, the possibility of a defect sneaking in undetected decreases.

3. **Feature Toggling**: This advanced technique allows developers to

hide, enable, or disable a feature during runtime, benefiting CD as it allows for feature testing in production without affecting the end users.

4. **Intensive Monitoring**: Monitoring application performance is essential in the CD pipeline. Tools like Splunk and DataDog help gather real-time application metrics, enabling quick resolution of issues.

4.5. Critical Considerations

While CD affords various advantages to the software development process, it's essential to evaluate the readiness of your team and project for such a change. Remember to consider whether the application requires frequent updates, if the team has the right set of skills, and whether your clients are ready for constant changes.

Continuous Deployment is a paradigm shift that can transform your organization's software lifecycle, making it more efficient and effective. While the journey might be challenging, its benefits in terms of improved product quality, faster delivery cycles, and quick response to client feedback justify the effort. Embrace CD, and usher in a new era of software development.

Chapter 5. Mastering the Code-Review-Deploy Cycle

The process of software deployment is often seen as a daunting waterfall of steps, from writing code to testing it, to getting it reviewed and fixing any discovered bugs, to ultimately deploying said code in a live environment. However, the advent of Continuous Integration and Continuous Deployment (CI/CD) pipelines hasn't just simplified this process, but also turbocharged it. Being a cornerstone of modern software development, CI/CD pipelines have proved instrumental in streamlining and accelerating the code-review-deploy cycle.

Let's have a deeper look into this cycle and unveil some strategies to master it.

5.1. The Anatomy of the Code-Review-Deploy Cycle

Before diving into the mastery of this vital cycle, it's fundamental to take a close look at its anatomy. The steps of this cycle, from writing to deploying code, operate seamlessly when well orchestrated with the logical principles that govern software creation.

In its simplest form, the 'code-review-deploy' cycle flows like this:

- Development of Code

- Code Review request

- Testing of Code

- Deployment

5.2. Harnessing the Power of CI/CD in the Code-Review-Deploy Cycle

CI/CD is more than just a buzzword; it's the lifeline of many modern software production pipelines. It's an essential tool in helping teams develop, deliver, and iterate on software with a quick and reliable feedback loop.

By integrating CI/CD into your process, you'll simplify and accelerate the entire code-review-deploy cycle. This way, the code is integrated (CI), tested, and deployed (CD) in continuous cycles, which ultimately leads to fewer errors, higher quality software products, and more efficient team productivity.

5.3. Best Practices for Development

The methodology of software development is akin to crafting art; there are many ways to sculpt, but the end product will always be a masterpiece if crafted with precision, care, and a meticulous understanding of the process.

To begin with, adopt a structured approach to scripting - following coding standards and clear naming conventions always help in the long run. Regularly commit updates to a shared repository to minimize integration hell and to ensure that everyone on the team is working on the latest codebase.

5.4. The Art of Code Review

Code reviews are one of the most instructive and constructive stages in the process of software creation. Not only is the reviewer put in a position to spot potential bugs, but also to identify areas of improvements or necessary refactors.

A good code review is prompt, thorough, and provides clear and actionable feedback. In addition, it is equally essential to embrace feedback from reviews and update your code accordingly. This iterative process enhances code quality and readability, improving overall project maintainability.

5.5. Intelligent Testing

In the CI/CD pipeline, testing is a continuous process integrated within the development process rather than a separate phase. Automated tests should be set up to run every time a change is made in the code repository.

Use different testing levels - unit tests for individual parts, integration tests for the whole system, and system tests to ensure the code works end-to-end in an environment that mirrors production. Additionally, adopt a test-driven development (TDD) approach, which ensures the software is always in a releasable state.

5.6. Streamlined Deployment

Up until the deployment phase, the development and testing environments ideally should mirror the production environment as closely as possible. During deployment, code is placed into the production environment, either manually or automatically.

CI/CD pipelines can automate this process, reducing the chances of human error. Moreover, this automated process reduces the release time from days to just a few minutes.

Remember, the end goal is to make deployments a 'non-event': regular, reliable, and as seamlessly integrated into the development process as possible.

5.7. Conclusion

By now, you should have a better understanding of the code-review-deploy cycle and how CI/CD pipelines can create transformative efficiencies. From adopting best practices and fostering an effective feedback loop, to integrating continuous testing and making deployments a 'non-event', mastering this cycle paves the way for high-quality, valuable software production.

As the software development landscape continues to evolve, remember that this mastery demands continuous learning, iteration, and growth. So, stay committed to refining your process, and harness the power of CI/CD to ultimately enhance the quality and efficiency of your software production.

Chapter 6. Case Studies: Improvements Introduced by CI/CD Pipelines

The rise of Continuous Integration and Continuous Deployment (CI/CD) pipelines in the software development world cannot go unnoticed, chiefly attributed to their overwhelming impact on quality, efficiency, and time management. This chapter presents various case studies, displaying the profound transformation that CI/CD pipelines have brought about within different organizations.

6.1. Case Study 1: Improving Developer Experience at Netflix

Netflix, renowned streaming service provider, integrated Spinnaker, their CI/CD tool, to power their incredible daily deployments – 4,000 times a day! This deployment power meant better customer experiences due to frequent updates and swift bug fixes.

Spinnaker has exponentially improved the developer experience by automating the tedious processes involved in code deployments. Incorporating CI/CD pipelines saved developers countless hours, freeing them to focus on creating quality features for the Netflix platform. Furthermore, Spinnaker's flexibility caters to Netflix's multi-cloud environment, making the collection and comparability of deployment metrics easier, thus perfecting their deployment systems.

6.2. Case Study 2: Boosting Release Pace at Etsy

Crafts marketplace, Etsy, utilized CI/CD pipelines to boost their release pace and code quality. Prior to the integration, deployments involved several risks and took inordinate amounts of time, often on a fortnightly basis.

Utilization of CI/CD not only gave a much-need boost to their deployment frequency (releasing multiple updates per day), but also reduced the code loop time. Quick feedback cycles resulted from continuous code integration, reducing error identification time and thereby improving the code quality extensively.

Moreover, Etsy experienced an exceptional reduction in configuration errors due to the mitigation of manual processes, further cementing the viability and worthiness of CI/CD pipelines.

6.3. Case Study 3: Update Rollbacks at Facebook

Facebook, with an ever-growing user base, found it challenging to manage their updates, often experiencing buggy rollouts and struggling with rollback processes. Integration of CI/CD pipelines addressed this issue.

By incorporating CI/CD concepts, Facebook managed to implement a 'one push' system where every update pushed into the production environment was reversible. This enabled smooth rollbacks in instances where the update failed or caused issues, without having to redeploy the entire application.

The 'one push' system, in turn, decreased downtime and improved the overall customer experience. The CI/CD pipeline's seamless automatic update rollbacks minimized potential disruptions and let the Facebook team concentrate fully on their product's quality and reliability.

6.4. Case Study 4: Frustration-Free Coding Experience at Microsoft

Microsoft sought to provide a seamless experience for developers working on Visual Studio, a popular IDE. They integrated the CI/CD philosophy into their workflow to address frequent build failures and extended bug fixing times, which often compromised programming productivity.

Microsoft's adoption of CI/CD led to improved build success rates and faster bug detection and fixes. Control and coordination of the deployment process advancements enabled Microsoft to deliver a more stable, reliable IDE to their developers. Furthermore, the process minimized productivity losses by enabling easier tracking, identification, and rectification of problems.

In these case studies, the merits of employing CI/CD pipelines clearly shine through. These industry giants, despite their diverse user bases and vastly different products, found a common solution in CI/CD pipelines. With CI/CD, they were able not only to streamline their software delivery process but also significantly enhance the quality of their products and services, thereby improving customer satisfaction and equipment efficiency.

Chapter 7. Troubleshooting CI/CD Pipeline Issues

Being an integral part of the DevOps mechanism, CI/CD pipelines are not devoid of issues or bottlenecks. While their benefits are numerous and significant, it's equally crucial to understand and address the potential pain points that may arise during their implementation and execution. Here, we delve into an exhaustive exploration of troubleshooting CI/CD pipeline issues, providing detailed strategies and tactics to prevent, diagnose, and resolve these problems.

7.1. Understanding CI/CD Pipeline Issues

CI/CD pipeline issues can range from minor glitches to major blockages that halt the entire software development and deployment process. The key to efficient troubleshooting is understanding the nature of these potential issues. Some common problems encountered while working with CI/CD pipelines include:

- Configuration errors

- Test failures

- Infrastructure issues

- Tool integration problems

- Security vulnerabilities

Each of these issues presents its unique challenges and requires a specific strategy for resolution. Understanding what causes them can significantly ease their troubleshooting.

7.2. Troubleshooting Configuration Errors

Configuration errors often arise from inaccuracies in setup files and incorrect environmental parameters. They may lead to pipeline failure even before the execution starts. Misconfiguration can result in inconsistent stages, incorrect trigger settings, or inappropriate branch selections.

To diagnose configuration errors:

- Inspect pipeline configuration files meticulously for any syntax, logic, or typographical errors.

- Examine if the environment variables and parameters defined match the intended configuration.

- Use configuration validation tools that indicate missing parameters or elements that breach the accepted schema.

For resolution:

- Correct any identified mistakes in the pipeline configuration files.

- Verify environment variables and parameters match the expected values and update if necessary.

- Utilize automated configuration testing to prevent configuration errors in the future.

7.3. Managing Test Failures

Test failures are one of the most common issues encountered in CI/CD pipelines. They affect both the integration and deployment processes. Failures could result from bugs in the code, incorrect tests, or changes in the application's environment.

To diagnose test failures:

- Review test results and logs for detailed error messages.
- Isolate the failing test cases and reproduce them locally if possible.
- Check recent changes in code that might have precipitated the test failures.

To resolve test failures:

- Fix the identified bugs in the code.
- Adjust or rewrite the incorrect tests.
- Constrain the testing environment to minimize uncontrolled variables that can influence test results.

7.4. Addressing Infrastructure Issues

Infrastructure issues can range from network instability and lack of storage space to incompatibilities in the operating systems. Such issues can disrupt the performance of a CI/CD pipeline and often require immediate attention.

To diagnose infrastructure issues:

- Monitor the performance metrics of the infrastructure.
- Check system logs and error messages related to hardware or network failures.
- Assess the system resources against the requirements of the pipeline processes.

To resolve infrastructure issues:

- Implement a robust resource management strategy to ensure adequate system resources are allocated to pipeline tasks.

- Regularly audit and update your infrastructure according to the pipeline requirements.

- Consider adopting infrastructure-as-code (IaC) practices for replicable, scalable infrastructure management.

7.5. Resolving Tool Integration Problems

Integration issues typically arise when tools used in the pipeline are incompatible, misconfigured, or outdated, leading to interrupted workflows.

To diagnose tool integration problems:

- Verify communication between different services through logs or console.

- Check for outdated versions of tools, plugins, or dependencies in your pipeline.

- Watch for inconsistent behavior between different environments.

For resolution:

- Update or replace outdated versions of tools.

- Check documentation and ensure tools are correctly configured as per instructions.

7.6. Mitigating Security Vulnerabilities

Security concerns in CI/CD pipelines exist where malicious code might be introduced or sensitive information leaked. These can have severe implications on the integrity and reliability of the pipeline and the resultant software.

To diagnose security vulnerabilities:

- Regularly scan your codebase and dependencies for vulnerabilities.

- Monitor access logs for unauthorized or suspicious activities.

- Audit your pipeline for potential data leakage points.

To mitigate these vulnerabilities:

- Strictly manage access controls and permissions.

- Implement security practices like secret management and automatic vulnerability scanning.

In conclusion, troubleshooting in CI/CD pipelines involves a recurring process of diagnosing and resolving issues. Remember, the key lies in proactive monitoring, timely intervention, and a deep understanding of your software development and deployment processes. Equipped with a robust troubleshooting plan, you are all set to make the most of your CI/CD pipeline, optimizing it for efficiency, quality and security.

Chapter 8. Making the Most of Modern CI/CD Tools

The advent of Continuous Integration and Continuous Deployment (CI/CD) pipelines has brought a paradigm shift in the realms of software development and delivery. Leveraging these modern tools, developers endeavor to mollify their processes, reduce bugs, and expedite feature rollouts. This chapter comprehensively dwells on how to procure optimal value from these advanced CI/CD tools.

8.1. Understanding CI/CD Tools

Continuous Integration (CI) is a software engineering practice where developers frequently merge their code changes into a central repository. Post integration, automated builds and tests are run to sustain code quality, detect problems early, and reduce integration costs. Continuous Deployment (CD), on the other hand, is an approach where every change that passes all stages of production pipeline is released to customers automatically, thus sustaining a rapid feedback loop with customers and reducing the time to market software products.

The CI/CD landscape presents a motley of tools, each offering unique features, and advantages tailored for specific use cases.

- **Jenkins**: An open-source automation server in which plugins allow the integration of every part of the DevOps lifecycle.

- **CircleCI**: This cloud-based tool provides powerful CI/CD environments, simple setup and maintenance, along with extensive language and platform support.

- **Travis CI**: Another hostable, cloud-based service, seamlessly integrated with GitHub.

- **GitLab CI**: An integral part of GitLab, conveniently offering a unified solution with a broad spectrum of features.

Understanding the functionalities that these tools offer is key to making an informed decision and integrating them appropriately into your software delivery workflow.

8.2. Integrating CI/CD Tools into the Workflow

Integration of CI/CD tools into the workflow is performed through a series of steps, paving the way for optimized production and operational efficiency.

1. Configure a Version Control System (VCS)

2. Fostering collaboration among Team Members

3. Setting up Automated Tests

4. Implementing the Integration and Deployment Tools

5. Monitoring and Logging the Operational Stages

8.3. Configuring a Version Control System

A Version Control System (VCS) allows developers to keep track of their code, changes, and adjust according to the project's requirements.

In respect to using CI/CD tools, it becomes especially crucial to keep your codebase in a VCS like Git, which will continuously integrate changes occurring over time. Once the repository has been set up, you can use a Webhook to trigger the CI/CD pipeline automatically whenever a new commit is pushed.

8.4. Fostering collaboration among Team Members

In an environment where multiple developers are working concurrently, communication and managing the changes efficiently are fundamental.

The team members should have well-defined roles, with each member aware of their specific responsibilities. Agile methodologies like Scrum and Lean can be helpful to manage tasks and boost productivity.

8.5. Setting up Automated Tests

Automated tests as part of your build pipeline are crucial for Continuous Integration. They ensure that every new change is validated automatically, without the need for manual intervention. The degree of your tests depends entirely on the complexity of your software, encompassing units, integration, and end-to-end tests.

8.6. Implementing the Integration and Deployment Tools

Choosing the right tools for integration and deployment is paramount. Here, 'right' mostly depends on the size of your project, the level of customization required, and your personal choice or compatibility with the tool. The setup of these tools includes installing them in your ecosystem and integrating with other tools utilized, like version control, collaboration, or monitoring tools.

8.7. Monitoring and Logging the Operational Stages

After the tools integration, a monitor setup tracks the performance. This stage includes observing the software's health, the progress of your CI/CD pipelines, and the application behavior once it has been deployed. In most cases, CI/CD tools provide extensive logging and auditing features, offering insights into successful and failed builds, reasons for failures, and time statistics.

Using such feedback, developers can turn it around to enhance their performance, resolve bugs quickly, thereby refining the entire process.

8.8. Conclusion

The integration and effective use of modern CI/CD tools determine the success of a software project to a great extent. A well-set workflow, combined with an appropriate set of tools, can ensure seamless software production, allowing development teams to deliver value more efficiently and quickly. Thus, understanding these tools, their features, the integration process, and how to optimize tools according to the specific projects can significantly enhance the output and efficiency of software delivery pipelines.

Chapter 9. Integrating CI/CD in Agile and DevOps

Adopting Continuous Integration/Continuous Deployment (CI/CD) within Agile and DevOps methodologies can streamline software development processes, enhance collaboration among teams, and accelerate the time-to-market for software products. Agile and DevOps, when coupled with CI/CD, have the capacity to realize better, faster, and more efficient software production.

9.1. The Intersection of Agile, DevOps and CI/CD

Agile methodology, which promotes iterative software development with constant feedback and incremental improvements, requires a structure within which continuous changes can be rapidly and effectively implemented. DevOps, an approach that bridges the gaps between development and operations, demands a seamless integration-mechanism to facilitate collaboration, code compatibility, and rapid deployment. This is where CI/CD pipelines fit perfectly, serving as the backbone of both Agile and DevOps methodologies.

With CI/CD pipelines, every code modification is automatically validated, integrated, and deployed, transforming the conventional, manual code-review-deploy cycle into an automated, streamlined process. It seamlessly bridges the divide between development and operations, fulfilling the core philosophy of DevOps as a mindset. All these attributes make CI/CD pipelines an indispensable part of Agile and DevOps methodologies, providing a platform for rapid, reliable, and effective software development.

9.2. The Role of CI/CD in Agile Development

Agile development, characterized by short, iterative development cycles called 'sprints', necessitates a continuous feedback mechanism to monitor and improve the process. An integral part of this iterative process is constant integration and testing, which is exactly what CI/CD pipelines offer.

CI validates each change in the codebase by automatically triggering a build and testing sequence. It ensures that the main codebase is always ready for deployment, while the Continuous Deployment (CD) takes the tested code and deploys it to production environments automatically.

Hence, CI/CD pipelines foster the iterative, feedback-driven Agile approach by:

1. Providing real-time feedback on the quality and stability of the code and immediately identifying issues.

2. Automating routine tasks such as testing, integration, and deployment, freeing developers to focus on problem solving and innovation.

3. Streamlining and accelerating the code-review-deploy cycle, which promotes rapid, incremental product improvement—a cornerstone of Agile methodology.

9.3. Implementing CI/CD in DevOps

In the DevOps era, the goal is to bridge the gap between development and operations, enabling continuous collaboration, integration, and deployment. CI/CD pipelines make this possible by ensuring that every piece of code is production-ready immediately after being committed.

In CI, each change made by developers is automatically integrated with the existing codebase. It's not only about merging the code; it's also about validating the changes through automated testing. This ensures the identification of bugs and inconsistencies early in the development cycle, mitigating the risk of introducing problematic code into the production environment.

On the other hand, CD picks up where CI ends. Once the code is tested and validated, CD ensures it's automatically deployed to the production environment. This results in a continuous, seamless flow, from coding to deployment—a central theme of DevOps.

By integrating CI/CD pipelines into DevOps, teams can:

1. Foster collaboration by establishing a single source of truth via shared code repositories.

2. Ensure a seamless flow from development to production via automated testing and deployment.

3. Accelerate feedback loop and issue resolution process by identifying the problems early.

4. Minimize machine-specific inconsistencies through a standardized integration process.

9.4. Challenges in CI/CD Implementation

While CI/CD pipelines hold immense potential for Agile and DevOps teams, implementing these processes isn't without challenges. Some common obstacles include:

1. The complexity of the CI/CD setup and configuration.

2. Resistance from team members unaccustomed to automated pipelines.

3. The need for extensive test coverage.

However, these challenges can be overcome with careful planning, positive reinforcement, and continuous team training.

9.5. Key Takeaways

CI/CD pipelines are not a mere tool but are integral parts of Agile and DevOps methodologies. They streamline and automate the development cycle, ensure code quality, foster collaboration, and ultimately, accelerate the software development flow. By embracing CI/CD in Agile and DevOps, businesses can realize faster time-to-market, enhanced product quality, and improved productivity, underscoring the importance of integrating CI/CD in Agile and DevOps environments.

Chapter 10. CI/CD Future Trends: A Glimpse Into the Crystal Ball

The realm of Continuous Integration and Continuous Deployment (CI/CD) is constantly evolving, with newer technologies and trends taking center stage unceasingly. Being aware and prepared for these shifts can give your organization an edge over competitions.

10.1. AI and Machine Learning in CI/CD

Artificial Intelligence and Machine Learning advancements are increasingly underway to disrupt CI/CD pipelines. These technologies promise to automate routine tasks, detect anomalies, predict potential risks, and optimize deployment strategies. AI can significantly facilitate test case management by automatically selecting the most pertinent test based upon the code changes.

ML assists in determining resource-intensive testing setup and deploys efficiently by dynamically responding to different workload requirements. They can learn from past data and behaviors to prevent potential bottlenecks and failures in the CI/CD pipeline.

Moreover, self-healing systems powered by AI/ML could proactively monitor and self-correct issues in the CI/CD pipeline. This self-correction allows developers to focus on growth-oriented tasks rather than issue resolution, improving overall productivity and efficiency.

10.2. Autonomous DevOps

The future trends point towards fully autonomous DevOps, which refers to the scenario with minimal human intervention. Task automation reduces risks associated with manual errors and ensures the consistency and reliability of software delivery. An autonomous CI/CD pipeline can manage and refine processes such as code integration, testing, deployment, and monitoring on its own.

Automation tools would take advantage of AI and predictive analytics to continuously analyze, learn, and adapt to changes, becoming smarter, faster, and more efficient over time. They would also auto-detect errors, alert the right personnel, and even propose resolution measures.

10.3. Infrastructure as Code (IaC)

Today, developers are increasingly relying on the Infrastructure as Code (IaC) paradigm, which treats infrastructure setup as software that can be versioned and tested, just like the application code. IaC can thus integrate into the CI/CD pipeline, allowing teams to apply continuous integration principles to infrastructure itself.

IaC democratizes the process and reduces dependency on any single team or person for environment configuration. It enforces consistency and repeatability, leading to an increased velocity in software delivery.

In the future, we can anticipate more mature approaches and tooling for IaC, which will make it more seamless and error-free, solidifying its position as an integral part of CI/CD pipelines.

10.4. Security Shifts Left

When it comes to software development, security is no longer an afterthought but an integral part of the CI/CD pipeline – a concept aptly named 'Shift Left'. By shifting security checks to an earlier stage in the process, problems can be identified and addressed before they escalate into costly and time-consuming issues.

In the future, as DevSecOps (a practice integrating security checks into the DevOps process) becomes a norm, we can expect more sophisticated security tooling, strategies, and best practices. These would allow organizations to develop secure software quickly without any compromise on the speed or quality of delivery.

10.5. Serverless Architecture

Serverless architectures are another promising trend in the CI/CD pipeline. They allow developers to focus on the coding part rather than the infrastructure, as the latter is managed by the serverless provider. This alleviates developers from tasks such as provisioning, scaling, or managing servers, and lets them concentrate on developing innovative solutions.

Serverless strategies provide scalability, efficiency, and high availability. In the future, serverless will continue to evolve, allowing even more complex applications to take advantage of it seamlessly.

Continuous Integration and Continuous Deployment (CI/CD) is a moving space with a plethora of innovative trends shaping its landscape. By preparing for these emerging trends, your organization can stay ahead, continuously improving efficiency and reliability in software development and deployment. Improvements in AI, automation, IaC, security, and serverless architectures promise an exciting future for CI/CD, one that redefines and streamlines processes while minimizing potential errors. Using these innovations can help you embrace new possibilities and achieve the full potential of your CI/CD pipeline.

Chapter 11. Frequently Asked Questions on CI/CD Pipelines

The CI/CD pipeline is a fundamental part of the software development process. It ensures the smooth and continuous progression of changes from the development stage, through several checks and balances, to the deployment stage in a controlled, automated and efficient manner. Here we will address the frequently asked questions about the CI/CD pipeline.

11.1. What is Continuous Integration?

Continuous Integration (CI) is a development practice where developers merge their changes into a main branch of a shared repository multiple times a day. Each change is then validated by creating a build and running automated tests against the build. This allows teams to detect problems early and resolve them more effectively.

11.2. What is Continuous Deployment?

Continuous Deployment (CD) is the process of deploying all changes that have been successfully validated in the CI step to the production environment, automatically and without human intervention. This ensures that any version of the software that passes all stages of the pipeline is production-ready and can be released at any time.

11.3. Why are CI/CD Pipelines Crucial in Application Development?

CI/CD pipelines play a central role in accelerating software delivery by reducing bottlenecks and enhancing code quality. They enforce testing in early stages, catching bugs sooner, and allowing faster recovery. Furthermore, they eliminate human error in repetitive tasks, cut costs, and encourage a culture of collaboration by integrating the work regularly.

11.4. How Does a Typical CI/CD Pipeline Work?

A typical CI/CD pipeline consists of several stages. First, the developer commits their changes to a shared repository. These changes trigger the pipeline, starting with the build stage wherein the application is compiled. Following that, the application passes through various test stages where it's checked for bugs and vulnerabilities. These might include unit tests, integration tests, system tests, acceptance tests, and security tests. If the application passes all tests, it moves to the deployment stage where it is brought live on the production environment. If the application does not pass a test, progress is halted and notification is sent to the development team.

11.5. What Tools are Used in CI/CD Pipelines?

There are several tools available to help implement CI/CD pipelines, each boasting a unique set of features. Jenkins, a widely used open-source tool, offers high modularity through its vast plugin ecosystem. GitLab can be a one-stop-shop, as it incorporates features pertaining to all steps of the pipeline. CircleCI excels at handling jobs within docker containers and parallel job execution, while TravisCI offers seamless integration with GitHub. Other popular options include Bamboo, TeamCity, and Azure DevOps, among others.

11.6. What are Some Common Challenges with CI/CD Implementations?

Some of the common challenges around implementing CI/CD pipelines include lack of knowledge and experience, resistance to cultural change, maintaining test data and environments, and managing a concurrent pipeline for multiple developments. Thus, having a comprehensive learning program, fostering a DevOps culture, maintaining test data integrity, and careful pipeline configuration are key to overcoming these challenges.

11.7. What are Best Practices for CI/CD Implementations?

Several best practices can help ensure an efficient CI/CD pipeline. These include maintaining a rigorous testing regime, keeping builds fast, using feature toggles to avoid broken functionality, maintaining a strong monitoring and logging system, and creating a culture of knowledge sharing. Applying these principles can significantly increase the success rate of CI/CD pipelines.

11.8. How Can I Measure Success in CI/CD Pipelines?

Success in CI/CD can be measured using a variety of key metrics. These might include deployment frequency, lead time for changes, failure rate of new deployments, and time to recover from failure. Examining these metrics can provide valuable insights into the effectiveness of the pipeline.

Remember, CI/CD pipelines are a journey, not a destination. They should continuously evolve with the needs of your team and the demands of your projects. Learning and curiosity are your allies on this journey, so keep asking questions and seeking answers!

www.ingramcontent.com/pod-product-compliance
Lightning Source LLC
Chambersburg PA
CBHW071012260726
48661CB00007B/2929